Are the Forks on the Table?

forks

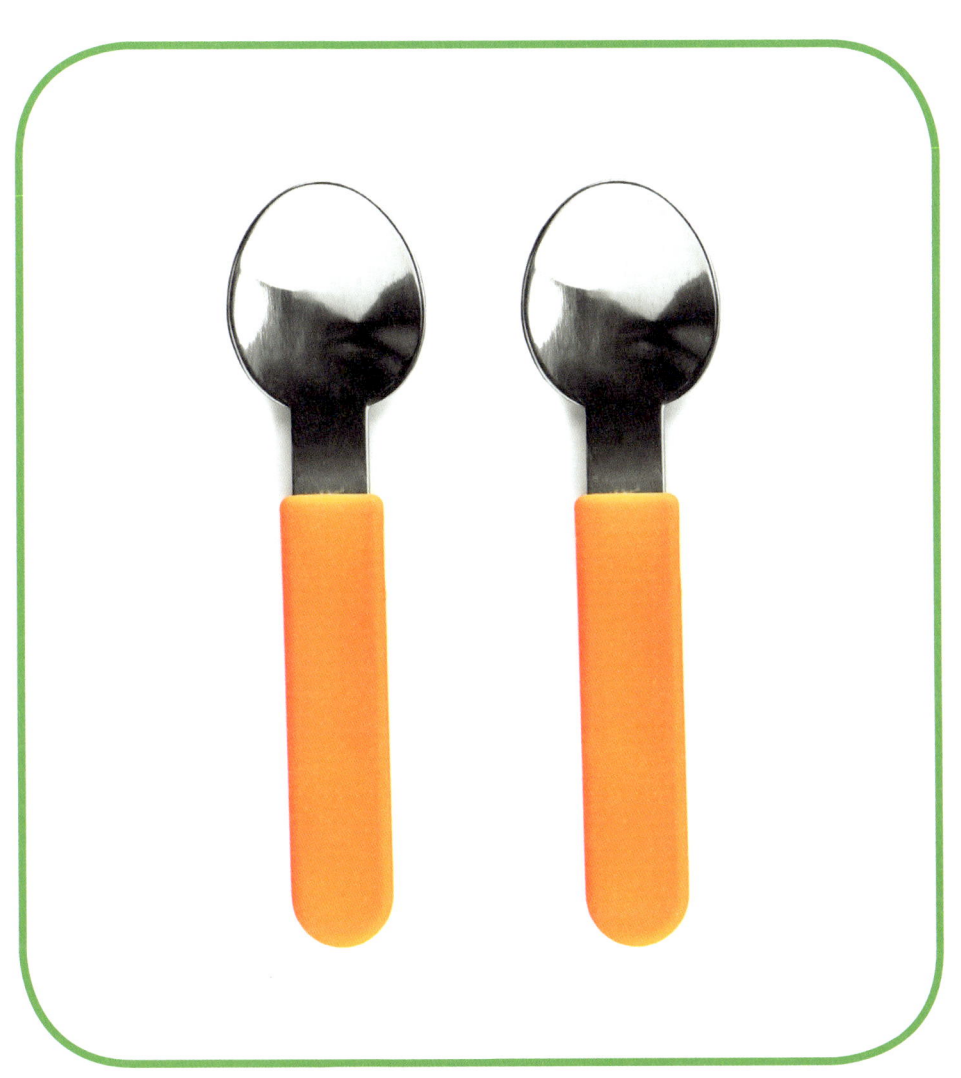

spoons

knives

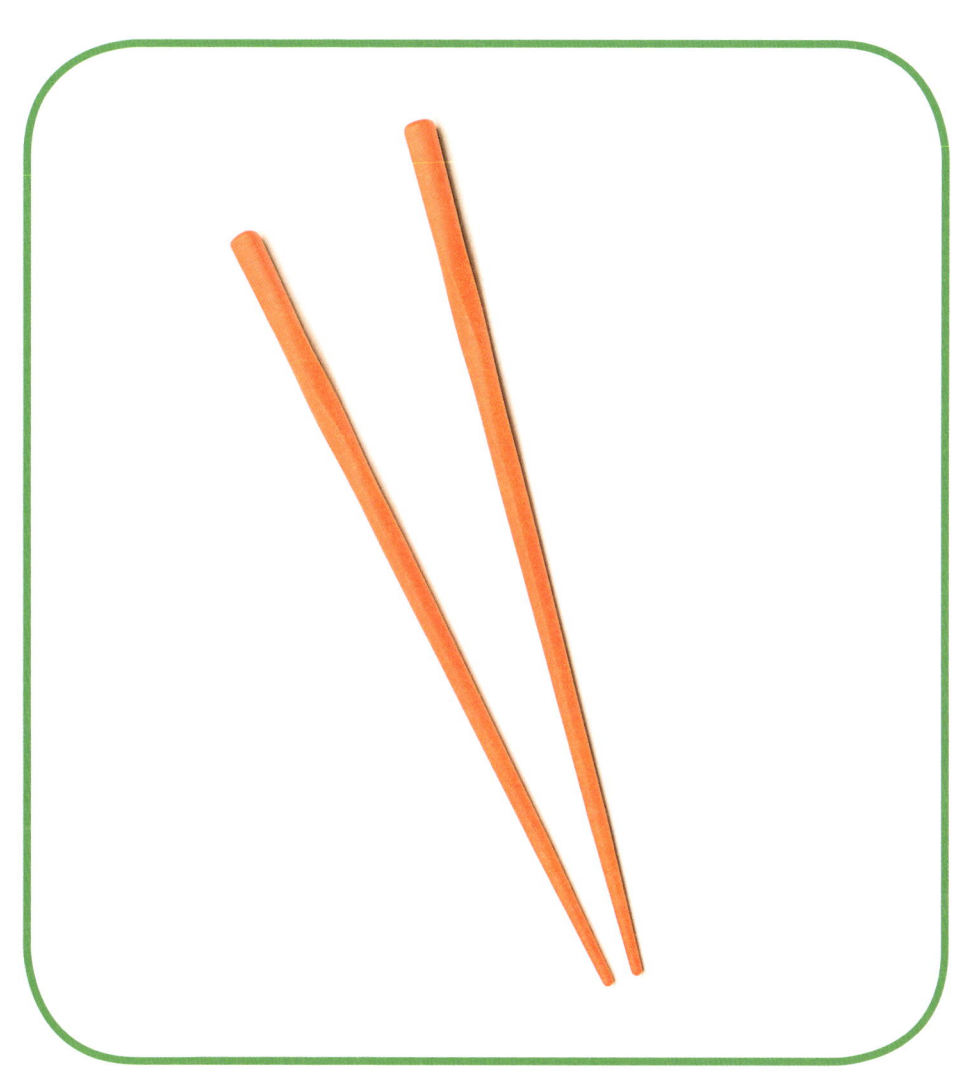

chopsticks

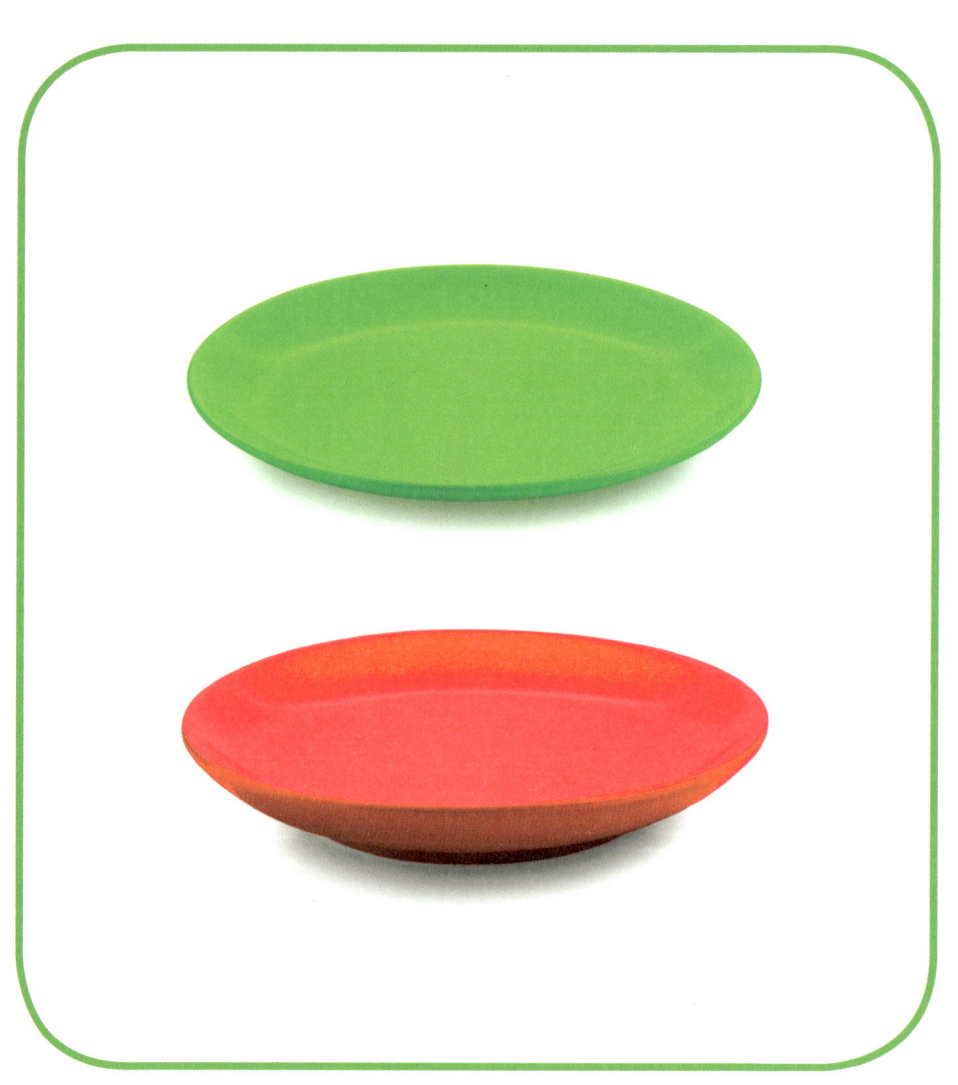

plates

bowls

cups

napkins

Are the forks on the table?

Yes, the forks are on the table.

Are the spoons on the table?

Yes, the spoons are on the table.

Are the knives on the table?

Yes, the knives are on the table.

Are the plates on the table?

Yes, the plates are on the table.

Are the napkins on the table?

Yes, the napkins are on the table.

Are the chopsticks on the table?

No, the chopsticks are not on the table.

Let's learn more about the Netherlands.

Stroopwafels